Level 2 ...

Accounting

Cover note

The purpose of this book is to simplify the course content, which I found to be confusing from time to time, as I was new to accountancy. This book does not aim to replace learning materials required for the course, however aims to break them down further, enabling students to already have effective notes at their disposal which will aid in learning and also making other learning materials such as flashcards, less time consuming.

I hope you enjoy this short book, as the notes taken have helped me through the exams, but please bear in mind I have focused solely on the tests when I have made these notes and not so much the reasons for why the methods are performed this way, I recommend you also source information from accredited books which our tutor will advise you of to better understand your course requirements, however I hope this book will aid you as it has me in understanding them.

Also note that the first module working in accounting and finance I not included as this is generally taught quite quickly by your tutor and focuses more on professionalism rather than the actual accounting methods learned later in the course. Same goes for sage, this book focuses on the hard to understand modules in level 2 accountancy.

Happy learning and good luck for your exams ☺

The costing system

The purpose of costing

- Costing or 'cost accounting' enables the managers of a business to know the firm's output – the revenues from sales from either a product or service. Once costing information is available, managers can use it to assist with decision making, planning for the future and the control of expenditure.

Cost accounting is widely used by

- A manufacturing business which makes a product e.g. a car

- A business that provides a service e.g. a holiday company

Being able to work out the cost of a product or service, the managers of an organisation can then use this to:

- Help determine the selling price

- Value inventory (stock) that the organisation holds

- Provide information for financial statements

- Make management decisions (for example about how many items should be made or sold)

What is a costing system?

A costing system is used by an organisation to collect information about costs and use that information for decision making, planning and control.

What is Financial accounting?

Financial accounting is concerned with recording financial transactions that have happened already and with providing information from the accounting records.

The main features of financial accounting are that it:

- Records transactions that have already happened

- Looks back to show what has happened in the past

- Is accurate to the nearest penny, with no estimated amounts

- It is often a legal requirement to keep accounts (for example in order to prepare VAT returns)
- Maintains confidentiality of information (e.g. payroll details, VAT returns)

What is management accounting?

Management costing (including costing) is concerned with looking at actual transactions in different ways from financial accounting. In particular, the costs of each product or service are considered both in the past and as the likely costs in the future.

In this way, Management accounting is able to provide information to help the business or organisation plan for the future.

The main features of management accounting are that it:

- Uses accounting information to summarise transactions that have happened already and to make estimates for the future

- Looks in detail at the costs and the sales income of products and services

- Looks forward to show what is likely to happen in the future

- May use estimates where these are the most suitable form of information

- Provides management with reports that are of use in running the business or organisation.

- Provides management information as frequently as circumstances demand – speed is often vital as information may go out of date very quickly

- Is not usually sent to people outside the organisation – it is for internal use

- Maintains confidentiality of information (e.g. payroll details)

Costs can be sub-divided into:

- Costs from the past – **Historic costs**

- Costs from the present – **Current costs**

- Costs for the future – **Future costs**

Financial accounting data – historic costs

The majority of financial accounting data has come from entering in the book keeping ledgers items such as:

- Invoices for sales and purchases

- Payments

- Receipts

- Payroll

This provides an accurate record of what has happened in the past, from this a business could find out:

- How much rent was paid in the last year

- What was the cost of paying wages last month

- How much was paid for materials in the last year

By looking beyond the ledger entries to the actual invoices and other financial accounting source documents, a business could also find out in more detail:

- How much the monthly rent was during each month of the last year

- How many employees there were last month and how much each grade of labour was paid

- How much was charged by suppliers for specific materials and what quantities were bought

Introduction to classifying costs and income

The elements of cost

All businesses or organisations incur costs – these can be broken down into:

- Materials

- Labour

- Expenses

Material costs

Material costs include the costs of:

- Raw materials and components bought for use by a manufacturing business

- Products bought for resale by a shop or wholesaler

- Service items or consumables, such as stationary, bought for use within a business or organisation

Labour costs

Refers to the payroll costs of all employees of the business or organisation. These costs include:

- Wages paid to those who work on the production line of a manufacturing business

- Wages and salaries paid to those who work for a manufacturing business but are not directly involved in the production line e.g. supervisors, maintenance staff, office staff, sales people.

- Wages and salaries of those who work in the service industry e.g. shops, banks, restaurants, accountants

- Public sector wages, e.g. of central and local government employees

Expenses

- A term that refers to the running costs of the business or organisation that cannot be included under the headings of materials and labour.

- The vast majority of expenses are also classified as overheads

Income

The main source of income in the private sector is from the sale of products or services. There may also be other, smaller amounts of income e.g. interest received on bank balances, rental income if part of the premises is let to a tenant, government grants or allowances for setting up a new business or buying new technology

Classification of costs by function and nature

The two main functions carried out in a manufacturing organisation are:

- The factory – where the goods are produced
- The warehouse and offices – where the support functions take place e.g. administration, selling and distribution and finance

Costs in the factory – production costs

Production costs can be divided into:

Direct costs – can be identified directly with each unit of output

Indirect costs – cannot be identified directly with specific units of output

The term unit of output refers to products that a manufacturer makes or services that are provided by a service organisation.

Direct Costs

- **Direct materials** – the cost of the materials used to make the items produced – for example the cost of the wood used to make chairs in a furniture factory

- **Direct labour** – the cost of paying the employees who carry out the production – for example the cost of paying the wages of workers making chairs in a furniture factory

- **Direct expenses**

Indirect production costs (production overheads)

- Indirect materials – the cost of materials that cannot be directly linked to specific items produced – for example the cost of replacement saw blades in a factory making furniture

- Indirect labour – the cost of employing people in the factory who do not actually make the products – for example the cleaners and supervisors in a furniture factory

- Direct Expenses - the other costs of running a factory – for example the heating and lighting costs

The total of production costs and indirect production costs is simply known as **total production costs**

Costs outside the factory – non – production costs

The non – production costs are divided into the functions of:

- Administration

- Selling and distribution

- Finance

Classification of costs – summary

Classification by element

- Materials
- Labour
- Expenses

Classification by function

- Production
- Administration
- Selling and distribution
- Finance

Classification by nature

- Direct costs
- Indirect costs

Cost centres and cost behaviour

Cost centres are sections of an organisation to which costs can be charged

Analysis of costs and different cost centres

By analysing costs, the information provided will be able to help the entre manager:

- To plan for the future

- To make decisions

- Control costs

The information comes from

- Purchase orders and purchase invoices, for materials and expenses costs

- Payroll schedules, for labour costs

- Bills and cash receipts, for expenses costs

Profit centres

Profit centres are sections of a business to which costs can be charged, income can be identified and profit can be calculated

Income (sales) − costs = Profit centre

Investment centres

Investment centres are sections of an organisation where information on income and costs can be gathered.

It can also gather information on the amount of the investment

Investment can take form of a non-current asset (fixed) and current assets (buildings, machinery, inventory etc.)

Coding systems

Numeric coding – comprised entirely of numbers

Alpha numeric coding – comprised of numbers and letters

Alphabetic coding – Comprised entirely of letters

Cost behaviour

Fixed costs – do not alter when the level of output or activity changes

Variable costs – change in proportion to the level of output or activity

Semi-variable costs – contain both a fixed element and a variable element

Inventory valuation and the manufacturing account

Inventory or stock is held by a range of businesses

- Trading organisations – buy and sell items; this is their inventory

- Manufacturers – hold inventory in a various forms; starting with raw materials, works in progress and lastly finished goods

Inventory valuation

Inventory valuation is required to calculate:

- The cost of items that have been used in the production process to make a finished product
- The costs of items that remain

Valuation methods

- FIFO – First in first out
  Means the stock which has been in stores the longest is used to value the inventory

- LIFO – Last in first out
  Means the stock which has been recently purchases is used to value the inventory

- AVCO – Average cost
  Total cost of goods in stores / Number of items n store = Average cost

Calculation of inventory valuations

<u>Cost of goods sold</u>

Opening inventory of raw materials

+

Purchases of raw materials

-

Closing inventory of raw materials

=

Direct materials used

+

Direct labour

=

Direct cost

+

Manufacturing overheads

=

Manufacturing cost

+

Opening inventory of work in progress

-

Closing inventory of work in progress

=

Cost of goods manufactured

+

Opening inventory of goods sold

-

Closing inventory of goods sold

=

Cost of goods sold

Labour costs

There are four main methods of calculating pay:

- **Time rate** – pay per hour

- **Overtime** – extra pay per hour

- **Bonus** – additional pay on performance

- **Piecework** – paid on items made

Direct labour costs

The pay which is paid to those who work directly with the manufacturing of the product

Indirect labour

The pay which is paid to those who do not directly work in the manufacturing of the product (supervisors, cleaners, selling ad distribution staff etc.)

Providing information and using spreadsheets

Unit cost reports

To calculate the unit cost you need to:

- Calculate the total costs for each category of cost (for example each element) based on the given production level

- Dividing these totals by the production level to arrive at unit costs for each category of cost

- Adding these unit costs together to arrive at the total unit cost

Budgets

A budget is a financial plan for an organisation that is prepared in advance

The purposes of a budget are:

- The budget creates plans

- The budget communicates and coordinates plans

- The budget can be used to monitor and control

<u>Calculating variances</u>

Adverse – the actual cost is greater than the budget cost

Favourable – the actual cost is less than the budget cost

Budget- actual = variance

If answer is positive the variance is favourable if the answer I negative the variance is adverse

<u>To calculate the percentage of a variance</u>

1) Variance / budget
2) X 100

Financial Transactions

Selling Goods and services

Goods and services can be sold:

- For Immediate payment (Cash Sales)
- For later payment (Credit Sales)

The five Stage accounting system

1) Financial Transaction
2) Financial Document
3) Books of Prime entry
4) Ledger Accounts
5) Trial balance

From Books of Prime entry to ledger accounts

Transaction – Sales Transaction

Book of Prime entry – Sales day book or sales returns day book

Ledger accounts – Customer sales →   debit

                                                             credit

                  Customer returns →   debit

                                                             Credit

Transaction – Purchases Transaction

Book of prime entry – Purchase day book or Purchase returns day book

Ledger accounts – Purchases from suppliers → debit

credit

                          Returns to suppliers →
debit

Credit

Transactions – Cash and Bank transactions

Book of Prime entry – Cash book

Ledgers – Payments received ⟶ debit

Payments made ⟶ credit

Transactions – Petty cash book

Book of Prime entry – Petty cash book

Ledgers – small cash payments made ⟶ debit

Cash received ⟶ credit

Financial Statements

- **Statement of profit or loss**
  Income – Expense = Profit
  Financial statement calculating profit (or loss) made by a business
- **Statement of Financial position**
  Assets – Liabilities = Capital
  Financial statement showing the value of the owner's investment

Terminology

Inventory = Stock

Trade Payable = Creditor

Trade Receivable = Debtor

Statement of profit or loss = Profit or loss account

Statement of financial position = Balance sheet

Financial Documents

Selling goods and services – the flow of documents

- Seller – Quotation or Catalogue sent
  Price Quotation given

- Buyer – Decision to buy; order placed
  Purchase order

- Seller – Order received, goods or services
  supplied, request for payment
  Delivery note
  Invoice

- Buyer – Goods received and checked; if faulty
  goods are returned
  Returns Note (Along with any faulty goods)

- Seller – Credit note authorised; request for
  payment
  Credit note
  Statement

- Buyer – Amount owing reduced by credit
  note; Payment made in due course

Purchase orders

- Each purchase order has a specific reference number; this is useful for filing and quoting on later documents, such as invoices and statements.

- The catalogue number of the goods required is stated in the product code column.

- The description of the goods is set out in full

- The price is not essential, although some purchase orders will include a price

- The purchase order is signed and dated by the person in charge of purchasing – without this authorisation the supplier is unlikely to supply the goods (the order will probably be returned).

Delivery Note - (Despatched with goods when order is ready)

- The delivery note has a numerical reference, useful for filing and later reference if there is a query.

- The method of delivery is stated

- The delivery note quotes the purchase order number; this enables the buyer to link the delivery with the original purchase order.

- The delivery note quotes:
1) Product code
2) Quantity supplied
3) Description of goods, but no price

- The delivery note will be signed and dated by the person receiving the goods as proof of delivery; nowadays this process can also be carried out electronically – the person receiving the goods will be asked to sign a portable electronic device.

Invoice

- The invoice is the trading document which is sent by the seller to the buyer stating how much is owed by the buyer of goods and services

- An invoice will normally be printed as part of a multiple set of documents which is likely to include a delivery note and a copy of the invoice for the sellers own records. The copy invoice will normally be filed in numerical order

- The Invoice shows the address of the seller of goods and services, where the invoice should be sent and where the goods should be sent.

- There are a number of important coding references on the invoice:

  1) The numerical reference of the invoice itself
  2) The account number allocated by the seller
  3) The original reference number on the purchase order, by the buyer; which will enable the shop to link the invoice with the original order.

4) The product code from the seller's catalogue or product list – Note: coding can be numeric or alpha-numeric.

- The date on the invoice is important because the payment date can be calculated from it. It is also the transaction date used for VAT purposes.

- The invoice must specify accurately the goods supplied. The details – set out in columns in the body of the invoice include:
1) **Product code** – this is the catalogue number which appeared on the original purchase order and on the delivery note
2) **Description** – The goods must be specified precisely
3) **Quantity** – You should agree with the quantity ordered
4) **Price** – This is the price of each unit shown in the next column
5) **Unit** - is the way in which the goods are counted and charged for
6) **Total** – is the unit price multiplied by the number of units
7) **Discount %** - is the percentage allowance (often known as 'trade' discount) given to customers who regularly deal with the supplier.

8) Discounts are also given for bulk purchases – bulk discount will also be shown in the discount column

9) **Net** – is the amount due to the seller after deduction of trade or bulk discount and before VAT is added on

Totals and VAT

- **Goods total** – is the amount due to the seller (it is the total of the net column)
- **Value added tax (VAT)** – at the minute is at 20% and is added to the goods total after the discounts have been taken
- **Total** – is the VAT plus the goods total, it is the amount owed to the seller.

Invoice Terms

- **Net monthly** – This means that the full payment of the invoice should be made within a month of the invoice date.

- **Carriage paid** – Means the price of the goods includes delivery

- **E&OE** – Stands for (errors & omissions expected), which means that if there is an error or something left off the invoice by mistake; resulting in an incorrect final price, the supplier has the right to rectify the mistake and demand the correct amount.

- **Settlement discount/ Cash discount** – is a further discount if payment is made within a specified timescale.

Credit note

- A credit note is a refund document reducing the amount owed by the buyer, reasons for refund by credit note may include:
  1) Damaged goods
  2) Goods that have not been sent = **shortages**
  3) The unit price on the invoice may be incorrect; overcharging the buyer

Statement – The seller requests payment

- A statement of account is sent by the supplier to the buyer at the end of the month.
- This statement shows what is owed by the buyer to the seller
- It contains details of:
  1) Any balances (**amounts owing**) at the beginning of the month – these appear in the debit column, with the wording 'balance b/f' (**balance brought forward**)
  2) Any payments received from the buyer (**Credit column**)
  3) Invoice issued for goods supplied – the full amount due, including VAT (**debit Column**)
  4) Refunds made on credit notes – including VAT (**Credit Column**)
  5) The running balance, and in the box at the bottom, the final net total for all items
  6) The bank details required for making payment by BACS or faster payments

How to Calculate trade and bulk discount

- Step 1 – Calculate the total price before discount
- Step 2 – Calculate the trade discount
- Step 3 – Calculate the net price before VAT
- Step 4 – Calculate VAT
- Step 5 – Calculate total invoice price

How to calculate Settlement (Cash) discount

- Step 1 – Calculate the total price before the trade discount
- Step 2 – Calculate the trade discount
- Step 3 – Calculate the net price/ goods total
- Step 4 – Calculate settlement discount
- Step 5 – Calculate the reduced goods total (do not write on invoice)
- Step 6 – Calculate VAT on lower amount
- Step 7 – Calculate the total invoice price (using the goods total before deduction of settlement discount)

Authorising and checking invoices

- In cases where a customer's credit limit has been exceeded, the invoice will need authorisation, from a more senior person in the accounts department.

- When checking an invoice, attention should be drawn to:
1) Purchase order relating to the invoice
2) The sellers own record of any price quoted
3) The sellers file record of the buyer
4) Is the correct customer being invoiced?
5) Are the goods being sent to the right place?
6) Are the correct goods being sent?
7) Is the quantity correct?
8) Is the unit correct?
9) Is the price correct?
10) Is the percentage discount being allowed to the customer?
11) Do any special terms apply?
12) Are the calculations on the invoice correct?

Discrepancies

<u>Internal checking process</u>

- Document passed back to the person or section, which made the mistake and a new corrected document will have to be issued and authorised; normally the original document reference number can be retained.

<u>External checking process</u>

- An apology should be sent to the buyer and correcting document issued; under no circumstances should the buyer alter or correct the document.

Double entry accounts

Financial Transactions – Financial Documents – Books of Prime entry – Entered in double entry

Double entry accounts record:

-   What is owed on credit by individual customers as a result of sales

-   What is owed on credit to individual suppliers as a result of purchases

-   Income items

-   Expense Items

Double entry accounts can be:

-   Accounts for types of income or expenses

-   Accounts for assets

-   Accounts for liabilities

How are double entry accounts organised?

Double entry accounts are grouped; for convenience into different ledgers:

- The ledger = Sales ledger + Purchases ledger + General ledger

- Sales ledger = accounts for customers who buy on credit, from the business; who owe money to the business

- Purchases ledger = accounts for suppliers; who supply on credit to the business and to whom the business owes money

- General ledger = Accounts for assets, liabilities, owners, capital, expenses and income

Double entry 'T' accounts

- Each 'T' account has two sides debit (Dr) on the left and Credit (Cr) on the right

Debits and Credit rules

Bank accounts
- Banks see a debit as a payment out of a bank account
- Banks see a credit as a payment into a bank account

Business accounts
- Businesses see a debit as a payment into the bank
- Businesses see a credit as a payment out of the bank

- Money paid into the bank results in a debit entry to the bank account in the accounting system of a business

- Money paid out of the bank results in a credit entry to the bank account in the accounting system of a business

Entries that are always debits:

1) Purchases
2) Expenses
3) Assets bought

Entries that are always credits:

1) Sales
2) Capital
3) Loans

Accounting for Credit sales and sales returns

Financial documents
- Sales invoice
- Credit note

Books of prime entry
- Sales day book
- Sales return day book

General ledger
- Sales account
- Sales return account
- Sales ledger control account
- VAT account

Sales ledger
- Subsidiary accounts
- Accounts of trade receivables

Day books for credit sales and sales returns
- Sales day book
- Sales returns day book

Reasons for using books of prime entry

- The totals from the books of prime entry can be checked before they are entered in the ledger accounts

- The use of books of prime entry for a large number of regular transactions, such as sales, means that there are fewer transactions to enter into the double entry accounts

- The work of the accounts department can be divided up

- One person can enter transactions in the books of prime entry, while another can concentrate on double entry accounts

Accounting system for credit sales

Goods sold on credit
- Invoice (financial document) issued

Sales day book
- Book of prime entry

General ledger – Double entry accounts
- Debit to sales ledger control account
- Credit to sales account and VAT account

Sales ledger – subsidiary accounts
- Debit to trade receivables (customers) accounts

Accounting system for sales returns

Goods sold on credit returned
- Credit note (financial document) issued

Sales returns day book
- Book of prime entry

General ledger – Double entry accounts
- Debit to sales returns account, VAT account
- Credit to sales ledger control account

<u>Sales ledger – Subsidiary accounts</u>
- Credit to trade receivables (customers) accounts

Process payments from customers

- When a customer who has bought goods or services on credit makes a payment of the account, the customer will send a remittance advice to the seller.

- Payment may be received by cheque or electronically through BACS or faster payments, the bank computer-based payment transfer systems

- When a remittance advice is received it must be checked carefully against the sales documentation held by the seller and the customer's account in the seller's sales ledger. The amount received must be the correct amount. The documentation checked includes invoices, credit notes and the remittance advice itself.

- If a cheque is received it must be checked to make sure it is valid

- If a payment is made through BACS or faster payments, the bank statement must be checked in due course to confirm that the payment has been received

- Discrepancies relating to payments received can be caused by
1) **Underpayments** – a disputed invoice may not have been included
2) **Overpayments** – A credit note may have been ignored or an invoice payed twice
3) Problems with the settlement account; discount rate incorrect, discount period expired, no discount available

- In all cases the discrepancies must be communicated to the customer so that an appropriate adjustment can be made

Process Documents from Suppliers

Ordering goods and services – the flow of documents

- Buyer – asks for price
  Price enquiry

- Seller – Price or catalogue sent
  Price quotation given

- Buyer – Decision to buy, Order placed
  Purchase order

- Seller – Order received, goods or services supplied
  Delivery note with goods
  Invoice

- Buyer – If goods are faulty they may be returned
  Returns note (sent with any faulty goods)

- Seller – Credit note authorised
  Credit note

- Buyer – Amount owing reduced by credit note

- Seller – Request for payment
  Statement

- Buyer – Payment made
  Remittance advice

Other ordering methods – paper based

- Filling in a catalogue order form and posting it to the seller with payment

- Telephoning a company which is selling to you for the first time to ask them to issue you with a 'pro-forma invoice' for the goods or services you need; when you receive this document, you will need to send this back with payment and the goods or service will be supplied in return.

- Faxing off a catalogue order form and quoting the company debit card or credit card details

- Telephoning an order and quoting the company debit or credit card details

Other ordering methods – Electronically based

EDI (Electronic data interchange)

- Connects businesses using a computer link so that documents such as purchase orders and invoices can be electronically generated and payments made electronically when they are due
- EDI has been running for years, the electronic links are private and secure; the system is expensive to set up. Supermarkets commonly use EDI

E-commerce (Electronic commerce)

- It covers selling and buying on the internet, both business to business and also by individual personal customers

  Note: financial documents are the same as chapter 2

Accounting for Credit Purchases and purchases transactions

Financial documents
- Purchases invoices
- Credit notes received

Books of prime entry
- Purchases day book
- Purchases returns day book

General ledger – double entry accounts
- Purchases accounts
- Purchases returns account
- Purchases ledger control account
- VAT account

Purchases ledger – Subsidiary accounts
- Accounts of trade payables (Suppliers)

Accounting system for credit purchases

Goods bought on credit
- Invoice (financial document) received

Purchases day book
- Book of prime entry

General ledger – double entry account
- Debit to purchases account and VAT account
- Credit to purchases ledger control account

Purchases ledger – Subsidiary accounts
- Credit to trade payables (suppliers) accounts

Purchase day book
- Purchase day book is prepared from financial documents – purchases invoices received from suppliers. The invoice number used is either that of the supplier's invoice or it is a unique number given to each invoice by the buyer's accounts department

- The code PDB57 is used for cross referencing to the book-keeping system; it would indicate that this is page 57 of the purchase day book (PDB).

- The account code column could cross reference by using 'PL'- the purchase ledger – followed by the account number of the trade payable (supplier).

- The total or gross column records the amount of each financial document after VAT has been included.

- The code 'GL' refers to the account numbers in the general ledger

- Purchase day ledger is totalled at appropriate intervals – daily, weekly or monthly and the total of the net column tells the business the amount of credit purchases for the period.

- The amounts from the purchase day book are recorded in the ledger accounts

In order to write up the purchase day book, we take purchases invoices; that have been checked and authorised – for the period and enter the details:

- Date of invoice

- Name of supplier

- Purchase invoice number, using either the suppliers invoice number, or a unique number given to each invoice by the buyer's accounts department

- Cross-reference to the supplier's account number in the purchases ledger

- Enter the total amount of the invoice into the totals column

- Enter the VAT amount shown on the invoice – don't be concerned with any adjustments to the VAT for the effect of any settlement (cash) discounts, simply record the VAT amount shown

- Enter the net amount of the invoice (often described as 'goods or services total') before VAT is added

Debit and credit example in purchases.

- Total of the 'total' column £480, has been credited to the purchases ledger control account (which records the liability to trade payables)

- The total of the VAT column, £80, has been debited to the VAT account (which has gained value)

- The total of the net column, £400, has been debited to the purchases account (which has gained value)

- Each entry in the general ledger is cross referenced back to the page number of the purchases day book.

Subsidiary accounts

- Subsidiary accounts are not part of double entry, but are represented in the general ledger by the purchase ledger control account, this mean that here a £480 credit entry could be split up in the purchases ledger into three different suppliers accounts

- Note that Subsidiary accounts are often referred to as memorandum accounts

Accounting system for purchase returns

- Goods returned to the supplier
Credit note (**Financial document**) received
from supplier

- Purchases returns day book
Book of Prime entry

- **General ledger** – double entry accounts
Debit – purchase ledger control accounts
Credit – Purchase returns account
VAT account

- **Purchase ledger**
Debit – trade payables (suppliers) accounts

Prepare Payments to suppliers

Reconciling the supplier statement of account

- The process of checking all purchase documentation for discrepancies is covered in chapter 6

The documents involved in this instance are:

- The delivery note's and the actual goods received (possibly using a goods received note)
- The supplier invoices and credit notes for calculation errors
- The supplier invoices and credit notes against the purchase order

Dealing with discrepancies

Problem – an invoice or credit note which appears on the supplier's statement, but for the wrong amount.

Cause & solution – the document will be held by the buyer and the amount can be verified, so this is likely to be an error made by the supplier when entering the amounts in the accounts; it will need to be queried by the buyer and investigated and put right by the supplier.

Problem – an invoice or credit note is on the supplier's statement and not in the buyers purchases ledger

Cause & Solution – This could be an invoice or credit note not posted to the buyers purchases ledger, or to the wrong suppliers account, by the buyer, this should be investigated and if there is an error by the buyer, included in the payment of account.

Problem – an invoice or credit note is in the buyer's purchases ledger and not in the supplier's statement

Cause & Solution – This could be an invoice or credit note not posted to the supplier's accounts, or posted to the wrong customer account by the supplier; this item should be queried by the buyer and if there is any error made by the supplier, included in the payment of account.

Problem – An invoice or credit note which appears twice on the supplier's statement

Cause & Solution – This is an obvious duplication of an invoice or credit note by the supplier (it does happen); the supplier should be notified of the error and the amount not included in the payment of account

The three Column cash book

There are two ways in which the cash book is used in the accounting system:

- Either the cash book combines the roles of a book of prime entry and double entry book keeping.

- Or the cash book is the book of prime entry only and a separate bank control account is kept in the general ledger in order to complete double entry book keeping.

Uses of the cash book

The cash book records the money transactions of the business, such as:

1) Receipts
- From cash sales
- From trade receivables
- Loans from the bank
- VAT refunds
- Capital introduced by the owner

2) Payments
- For cash purchases
- To trade receivables

- For expenses
- For bank loan repayments
- For VAT Payments
- For the purchase of non – current assets eg vehicles, office equipment
- For drawings (Money taken by the owner of the business for personal use)

The cash book is controlled by the cashier who:

- Records, receipts and payments through the bank

- Makes payments and prepares cheques and bank transfers for signature by those authorised to sign

- Pays cash and cheques received into the bank

- Has control over the business cash – in a cash till, cash box or safe

- Issues cash to the petty cashier who operates the petty cash book

- Checks the accuracy of the cash and bank balances at regular intervals

<u>The cashier is responsible for:</u>
- Issuing receipts for cash (and sometimes bank transfers) received

- Making authorised payments in cash and by cheque/ bank transfer against documents received (such as invoices or statements) showing all amounts due

<u>Accounting procedures must include:</u>

- Security – of cash, cheque books and internet banking, the correct authorisation of payments

- Confidentiality – that all cash/ bank transactions, including cash and bank balances, are kept confidential

Layout of the three column cash book

- This layout includes both the bank account and the cash account (used for cash kept on the business premise.

- The cash and bank Columns on the debit side are used for money in, ie receipts

- The cash and bank columns on the credit side are used for money out, ie payments

- A third money column on each side is used to record settlement discount (that is, an allowance offered for quick settlement of the amount due, eg 2% cash discount for settlement within 7 days).

- The discount column on the debit side is for settlement discount allowed to customers

- The discount column on the credit side is for settlement discount received from suppliers

- The discount columns are not part of the double entry system – they are used in the cash book as a listing device or memorandum column. They are totalled and transferred into the double entry system.

- The account code column is used to code or cross reference to the other entry in the ledger system.

Analysed cash book

An analysed cash book divides receipts and payments between a number of analysis columns, such as:
- 1) Receipts
- Cash sales
- VAT on cash sales and other income
- Receipts from trade receivables in the sales ledger
- Other income

- 2) Payments
- Cash purchases
- VAT on cash purchases and other expenses
- Payments to trade payables in the purchases ledger
- Other expenses, including dealing with dishonoured (bounced) cheques

Points to note about analysed cash books
- The analysed cash book analyses each receipt and payment between a number of headings. A business will adapt the cash book and use whatever analysis columns suit it best.

- For transactions involving receipts from trade receivables and payments to trade payables, no amount for VAT is shown in the VAT

Columns. This is because VAT has been charged on invoices issued and received and was recorded in the VAT account (via the day books) when the sale or purchase was made.

- The cash and bank columns are balanced in the way described in the previous chapter

- The discount columns are totalled at the end of the week ready to be transferred to the double entry system

Reasons Cheques may go dishonoured

- The cheque may be 'stopped' by the customer

- There may be something technically wrong with the cheque, for example not being signed

- The person issuing the cheque may not have enough money in their bank account, in this case the cheque will be marked 'refer to drawer', this is bad news for the business owed the money as it often means the customer is in financial difficulty.

How the cash book fits into the accounting system

- As well as being a book of prime entry, the cash book can perform the function of being a double entry account, i.e. a debit entry in the cash book can be a credit entry in another account.

- The cash book can also be treated solely as a book of prime entry, in which case separate double entry accounts – called **cash control account** and **bank control account** – are used in the general ledger

Petty cash book

Uses of the petty cash book

The petty cash book records the low-value cash payments for purchases and expenses of the business, such as:

- Stationary items

- Small items of office supplies

- Casual wages

- Window cleaning

- Bus, rail and taxi fares incurred on behalf of the business

- Meals and drinks incurred on behalf of the business

- Postages

- Tips and donations

The petty cash book is the responsibility of the petty cashier who:

- Receives an amount of money (known as the petty cash float) from the cashier to be used for petty cash payments

- Is responsible for security of the petty cash money

- Makes cash payments against authorised petty cash vouchers

- Records the payments made and analyses them in the petty cash book

- Receives and records any small amounts of income, e.g. postage stamps sold to staff for their private use

- Balances the petty cash book at regular intervals, usually weekly or monthly

- Tops up the petty cash float by claiming reimbursement from the cashier of the amounts paid out

- Passes the completed petty cash book to the book keeper so that data can be transferred into the ledger system

Petty cash vouchers

Petty cash voucher s are financial documents used by the petty cashier to write up the petty cash book, they contain the following:

- The date, details and amount of expenditure

- The signature of the person making the claim and receiving the money

- The signature of the person authorising the payment, normally the petty cashier, or a manager if the amount is higher than the authorisation limit

- Additionally, the petty cash vouchers are numbered, so that they can be controlled, the number being entered in the petty cash book

- With the relevant documentation, such as a receipt from a shop or post office etc. attached to the petty cash voucher.

Layout of the petty cash book

- There are columns showing the date and details of all receipt s and payments

- Receipts are shown in the debit column on the extreme left

- There is a column for the petty cash voucher number

- The total payment (i.e. the amount paid out on each petty cash voucher) is in the next column, which is the credit side of the petty cash book

- Then follow the analysis columns which analyse each transaction entered in the 'total payment' column

Control of petty cash

1) On taking over the petty cashier should check that the petty cash book has been balanced and that the amount of cash in the tin agrees with the balance shown in the book, if there is a discrepancy the accounts supervisor should be informed immediately.

2) The petty cashier should ensure each week or month is started with the imprest amount of cash which has been agreed with the accounts supervisor.

3) The petty cash is to be kept secure in a locked cash box and control kept of the keys

4) Petty cash vouchers (in number order) are to be provided on request

5) Petty cash paid out against correctly completed petty cash vouchers after checking that:
- The voucher is signed by the person receiving the money
- The voucher is signed by the person authorising the payment (the petty cashier or manager)

- A receipt or other supporting evidence is attached to the petty cash voucher and that the receipt and petty cash voucher are for the same amount
- The amount being claimed is within the authorised limit of the petty cashier

6) The petty cash book is written up (to include calculation of VAT amounts when appropriate); it is important that the petty cash book is accurate.

7) Completed petty cash vouchers are stored safely – filed in numerical order. The vouchers will need to be kept for at least 6 years. They may be needed by auditors or in the event of other queries. Completed petty cash books will also need to be retained.

8) A surprise check of petty cash will be made by the accounts supervisor – at any one time the cash held plus amounts of petty cash vouchers should be equal to the imprest amount.

9) At the end of each week or month the petty cash book will also have to be balanced

10) Details of the totals of each analysis column are given to the person who looks after the double entry accounts so that the amount of each expense can be entered into the double entry system.

11) An amount of cash is drawn from the cashier equal to the amount of payments made, in order to restore the imprest amount.

12) The petty cash book and cash in hand are to be presented to the accounts supervisor for checking

13) Any discrepancies are to be dealt with promptly; these may include:

- Petty cash claims not authorised

- Insufficient supporting evidence (eg missing receipt) attached to the petty cash voucher

- Amounts being claimed which exceed the authorised limit of the petty cashier

- A receipt and petty cash voucher total differing – the matter should be queried with the person who made the purchase

- A difference between the totals of the analysis columns and the total payments column in the petty cash book – check the addition of the columns, figures against the vouchers, the VAT calculations (does the VAT plus the analysis column amount equal the total payable amount).

- A difference between the cash in the petty cash box and the balance shown in the petty cash book – if this is not an arithmetic difference it may be a case of theft, and should be reported promptly to the accounts supervisor.

- Where discrepancies and queries cannot be resolved, they should be referred to the accounts supervisor.

How the petty cash book fits into the accounting system

In accounting the petty cash book is:

- Either a book of prime entry for low-value cash payments and the double entry account for petty cash (kept in the general ledger)

- Or the book of prime entry only, with a separate petty cash control account, kept in the general ledger in order to complete the double entry book keeping

Petty cash payments in the accounting system

Financial documents
- Petty cash vouchers for low value purchases and expense payments

Book of prime entry – Petty cash book
- Entries recording low value purchases and expense payments

Double-entry book keeping – petty cash book
- Debit – VAT account with total of VAT analysis column
- Debit – appropriate expense account with the total of each analysis column

- Credit – Petty cash payments column

The initial trial balance

A trial balance is a list of the balances of every account from the general ledger (including cash book and petty cash book), distinguishing between those accounts which have debit balances and those which have credit balances.

Notes on the trial balance

- The debit and credit columns are totalled and the totals should agree. In this way the trial balance proves that the accounting records are arithmetically correct

- The balance for each account listed in the trial balance is the amount brought down after the accounts have been balanced

- The order of accounts within the trial balance could be set out
1) In alphabetical order
2) In random order
3) In the order of final accounts, that is income and expenditure items from the income statement, followed by an asset, liability and capital items from the statement of financial position

Debit and credit balances

<u>Debit balances – Purchases, Assets, customer credit accounts (SLCA), Expenses, Drawings (PACED) TR</u>

- Purchases account

- Sales returns account

- Non – current asset accounts e.g. premises, motor vehicles, machinery, office equipment etc

- Inventory account – the inventory valuation, usually at the beginning of the year

- Expenses accounts, e.g. wages, telephone, rent, discount allowed

- Drawings account

- Sales ledger control account (which records the total balances of trade receivables)

- Petty cash control account

<u>Credit Balances – Sales, Capital, Income, Liabilities, Supplier credit account (PLCA) (SCILS) TP</u>

- Sales account

- Purchase returns account

- Income accounts e.g. rent received, commission received, fees received, discount received

- Capital account

- Loan account

- Purchases ledger control account

Notes
- <u>Bank control account can be either debit or credit – it will be:</u>
  1) Debit when the business has money in the bank
  2) Credit when it is overdrawn

- <u>Value added tax (VAT) account</u>
  1) Debit when VAT is due to the business
  2) Credit when the business owes money to HM Revenue and customs

Capital and revenue expenditure

Capital expenditure

- Delivery of non-current assets

- Installation of non-current assets

- Improvement (but not repair) of non-current assets

- Legal costs on buying property

An example of capital expenditure is the purchase of a car for use in the business

Revenue Expenditure

- Purchases made by the business

- Maintenance and repair of non-current assets owned by the business

- Administration of the business

- Selling and distributing the goods or products in which the business trades

An example of revenue expenditure is the purchase of fuel for the car used in the business

Capital Income

- Capital income is received form 'one off' transactions

- Sales of non-current assets

- Loans raised from banks and other lenders

- Capital or increases in capital, paid in by the owner of the business

Revenue income

- Revenue income is income received from the sales made by the business and other regular amounts of income

- Sales made by the business

- Rent from business premises rented out

- Commission for work done by the business on behalf of their businesses

- Cash discount for prompt settlement of amounts due to suppliers

Banks, building societies and payment systems

What is the difference between banks and building societies?

- A bank is a limited company owned by shareholders

- A building society is a 'mutual' owned by its members/ customers

Building society services

- Current and savings accounts for its members

- Mortgages for house purchase

- Some larger building societies may offer property linked loans for projects

Bank services

- **Current accounts** – dealing with cash, cheques and automated payments

- **Deposit accounts** – paying interest on surplus funds

- **Overdrafts** – flexible borrowing on a current account to cover temporary requirements

- **Loan accounts** – financing loans with flexile payments

- **Mortgages** – loans for property purchase

Bank services for the business owner
<u>Business current account</u>
- A working account through which day to day financial transactions pass, including payments received from customers and payment of business expenses and wages

<u>Deposit account</u>
- A deposit account is used for excess money held by a business and interest is paid by the bank on the amount deposited. Current account facilities such as cheques, standing orders, direct debits and overdrafts are allowed on deposit accounts.

- Substantial sums of money (normally £500,000 plus) are stored in treasury accounts, these accounts may allow

immediate withdrawal or require up to 6
months for a withdrawal.

Overdraft
- An overdraft is borrowing money from the
  bank from a current account, interest will
  only be charged on the amount borrowed.

Business loan
- A business loan finances large purchases,
  such as new machinery

- Loan amounts can range from £1,000 to
  £100,000

- Interest is paid either at a fixed rate at the
  beginning of the loan or a variable rate in line
  with market rates

- A loan is for a set time period between 2 and
  30 years

<u>Commercial mortgage</u>

- A commercial mortgage is a loan for up to 25 years to cover the purchase of a property

- Amounts range from £25,000 to £500,000

- Banks can provide up to 70% of a properties market value

- Interest is paid either a fixed or variable rate (the same as a loan would be)

<u>Other bank services for companies</u>

<u>Debit and credit cards</u>

- Issuing company credit cards, processing card payments as a merchant

<u>Insurance</u>

- Protection for business employees, premises and other risks

<u>International services</u>

- Currency accounts, overseas payments, dealing with export and imports

<u>Subsidiary companies owned by the banks may also help finance businesses through:</u>

- Leasing – a leasing company buys an asset from a business then rents that asset back to that business i.e. company cars etc.

- Factorising – invoices are effectively bought from the business that issues them and the factorising company then collects the money from the customer when credit is due.

Cheques

A cheque is an order in writing and signed by the customer (the drawer) telling the bank to pay an amount to someone (the payee)

When issuing a cheque, check the following details:

- Correct date

- Name of the payee

- Amount in words

- Amount in figures

- Authorized signature

- Counterfoil (date, amount, payee)

<u>Cheque clearing – 2,4,6 cycle (working days)</u>

- **Day 2** – interest on that amount will be paid on the amount paying in
- **Day 4** – the amount can be withdrawn from the account
- **Day 6** – the amount is guaranteed safe and the cheque cannot bounce

Payments by plastic card

Debit card – payment is taken straight away

Credit card – where payment is made by the customer to the credit card issuer at a later date than the purchase

Prepayment card – where a customer has already 'topped up' the card to a certain value and payment is taken from that value

The electronic methods used to process the payments are as follows:

- **Chip and PIN technology** – where a customer enters a PIN (Personal Identification Number)

- **Radio Technology** – where a customer pays by tapping or swiping the card at a terminal

- **A terminal or web link** – where the customer is not present and the transaction is mail order or online purchase, proceeded remotely using the card details provided by the customer

Bank Giro credits

- A little like a paying in slip and clears through a 3 day clearing system

BACS (Bankers Automated Clearing Services)

- A payment system owned by the banks
- The transfer is set up on a computer file and transferred between the banks
- Takes 3 working days to clear

BACS Direct credit

- Used for paying in wages or making payments to established suppliers on a monthly basis
- Takes 3 working day to clear

Faster payments

- Makes same day payments; usually two hours

Standing orders

- Can be set up via BACS or faster payments
- Used to make regular payments of the same amount

BACS Direct Debits

- For making a large amount of variable payments

Mobile electronic payments – future developments

- Allows owners of smart phones to download an app and after clearing security make payments on their mobile which will be processed as faster payments

One off large payments

CHAPS (Clearing House Automated Payments System)

- Cannot be cancelled once made
- Used for high cost like purchase and sale of property

Bank drafts

- A cheque written out by the bank, which is a guaranteed payment (as good as cash)
- Cannot be stopped once made

Payment cycles and the bank balance

Payment received

- The date the money will be cleared on the bank account and be used for expenses or earning interest

Payment made

- The date that the payment will leave the bank account and reduce the amount of money available

Filing retention policy

- 6 years plus the current year

Destruction of records

- Paper must be destroyed or shredded
- Electronic data must be wiped

Making payments

Outgoing payments

Issue of cheques

- Paying suppliers by cheques for goods or services

- Paying one off costs/ items of capital expenditure

- Paying bills by cheque or bank giro transfer

Paying by electronic transfer

- Paying wages

- Paying suppliers for goods and services

- Paying bills

Paying trade suppliers

A suppler is paid when:

- All documents such as the purchase order, delivery note (or goods received note) and invoice have been checked against each other (these are normally filed together)

- Any credit due e.g. for returned goods has been received in the form of a credit note

- All discounts, whether settlement (cash) discount or trade discount or bulk discount have been allowed for

- The payment has received the necessary authorization

AUDDIS (Automated Direct Debit Instruction Service) and the paperless direct debit

AUDDIS is used:

- To set up direct debits from customers without using paper
- By businesses to send a written copy to banks for validation (this is only part paperless)

Incoming payments

Payments can be received by:

- Cash
- Cheques
- Credit and debit cards
- Electronic inter-bank transfer (BACS, faster payments, CHAPS)

Tills and cash floats

Cash float at start of day + cash from sales made from day (listed on till roll) = cash held at the end of the day

Guidelines for cash handling

- Cash should be kept in a cash till or cash box (locked) when not in use

- The keys should be retained under the control of the cashier

- As little cash as practically possible should be kept in the tills

- Cash should be paid into the bank as soon as possible

Returned cheques

-   RD (refer to drawer) – means the customer has no money in the bank, you'll need to contact them for an explanation

-   RDPR (refer to drawer, please represent) – means there was no money in the bank but the cheque has been sent through clearing again (represent) in hope that it would clear

-   Payment countermanded by order of drawer – the cheque has been stopped by the customer

-   Technical issues – such as incorrect date, amount etc.

Chip and PIN

Chip and PIN was introduced:

-   To save time at the checkout

-   Safer means of payment

-   Removes the need for telephone calls to be made for authorization

Mail order/ telephone sales – customer not present

When accepting payment by debit or credit card the following details must be obtained

- The card number, 3-digit security code and expiry date

- The issue number and/ or start date of a debit card

- The name and initials of the card holder as shown on the card

- The card holders card statement address

- The card holders signature (mail order only)

Internet sales – customer not present

When purchasing online the customer will need to provide the following details:

- The customer's name

- Card address and delivery address (if different)

- Card details; card number, expiry date and security code

- Issue number and/ or start date of any debit card

Customer present – sales requiring a signature

- In the case of a shop till, swipe the card through the card reader

- The merchant's system checks that the card has enough money and is not lost or stolen

- If all is well the transaction will be passed through if not the customer will be asked to pay another way

- If the amount is above the floor limit a telephone call to the card merchant will be needed to authorize the transaction

- The till produces a two-part receipt which includes a space for the card holders signature

- The customer signs and the signature is compared to that on the card

- The customer is handed the top copy of the receipt and the other is kept for future queries

The following are checks that need to be made when authorizing a payment by signature

- The card has the appropriate logo

- The card has a magnetic strip on the reverse of the card

- The card has not expired

- The signature is consistent with the signature on the card

Mechanical 'push-pull' imprinter machine

- Check the card has not expired and place it on the imprinter

- Imprint the sales voucher by hand on the 'push-pull' imprinter

- Complete the sales voucher with date, details of goods and the amount

- The customer signs the imprinted sales voucher and the signature should be compared with that on the card

- If the payment is over the floor limit, the card merchant will need to be called for authorization

- The top copy of the sales voucher is handed to the customer and the other 3 copies are retained

- Of the 3 copies retained, the white one is treat like a cheque and the other two copies (yellow and blue) are retained for future queries

Paying into the bank

Importance of paying in promptly

- Theft
- Time-scale – security and cash flow
- Procedures
- Confidentiality

Bank statements

A bank statement is a summary showing

- The balance of the account at the beginning of the statement
- Amounts paid into that account
- Mounts paid out of the account

Double entry

Business customer

- Debit = money received
- Credit = Money paid out

Bank

- Debit = money paid out of a customer's account

- Credit = money paid into a customer's account

Bank reconciliation statements

Receiving a bank statement

When receiving a bank statement, it must be compared against the cash book to identify discrepancies, the differences will likely be:

1) Timing differences
- Unpresented cheques, i.e. cheques issued, not yet recorded in the bank statement
- Outstanding lodgements, i.e. amounts paid into the bank, not yet recorded on the bank statement
2) Updating items for the cash book

Preparing a bank reconciliation statement

- From the bank columns of the cash book, tick off, in both cash book and bank statement, the receipts as they appear in both

- From the bank columns of the cash book, tick off, in both cash book and bank statement, the payments as they appear in both

- Identify the items that are unticked on the bank statement and enter them in the cash book on the debit or credit side as appropriate. (do not enter an error in the cash book, instead inform the bank to rectify the error, the amount will need to be entered on the bank reconciliation statement)

- The bank columns are now balanced to find the up to date balance

- Start the bank reconciliation statement with the final balance figure shown on the bank statement

- In the bank reconciliation statement deduct the unticked payments shown in the cash book – these will be unpresented cheques

- In the bank reconciliation statement, add the unticked payments shown in the cash book – these are outstanding lodgements

- The resulting money amount shown on the bank reconciliation statement is the balance as per the cash book

Dealing with unusual items on bank statements

Out of date cheques

- The bank will not pay a cheque more than 6 months old so these will need recording properly in the cash book

Returned (dishonoured) cheques

- These should be entered in the cash book as a credit and as a debit to the sales ledger control (if it is a credit sale) and a debit to trade receivables account in sales ledger
- Or a debit to sales account (if it is a cash sale)

Bank errors

- A cheque being deducted from the bank account which has not been issued by the business

- A BACS receipt shown on the bank statement for which the business is not the correct recipient

- Standing orders or direct debits being pad at the wrong time or the wrong amount

Importance of bank reconciliation statements

-   Errors in the cash book or bank statements can be found and corrected

-   Assists in deterring fraud

-   The business has an amended figure for the bank balance to be shown in the trial balance

-   It is good practice

Using control accounts

The sales ledger control account

-   The sales ledger control account acts as a totals account
-   The sales ledger control account is reconciled with the balances of subsidiary accounts which it controls
-   Only credit sales and not cash sales are recorded in the sales ledger control account because only credit sales are recorded in the customer's accounts

Dishonoured cheques

- Debit sales ledger control account
- Credit cash book (bank columns)

Irrecoverable debts written off

- Debit irrecoverable debts account

- Debit VAT account

- Credit sales ledger control account

Information sources for sales ledger control accounts

- **Total credit sales (including VAT)** – from the total column of the sales day book

- **Total sales returns (including VAT)** – from the total column of the sales returns day book

- **Total cash/ cheques received** – from the customers in the analysed cash book

- **Total settlement discount allowed** – from the discount allowed column of the cash book or from the discount allowed account

- **Irrecoverable debts** – from the journal or irrecoverable debts written off account

The purchases ledger control accounts

<u>Information sources for purchases ledger control account</u>

- Total credit purchases (including VAT) – from the total column of the purchases day book

- Total purchases return (including VAT) – from the total column of the purchases returns day book

- Total cash/ cheque paid to suppliers – from the total column of the purchases returns day book

- Total settlement discount received – from the discount received column of the cash book, or from discount received account

The Journal

The journal is a book of prime entry for non-regular transactions which include:

- Opening entries
- Irrecoverable debts written off
- Payroll transactions
- Correction of errors

The reasons for maintaining the journal are:

- To provide a book of prime entry for non-regular transactions

- To eliminate the need for remembering why non-regular transactions were put through the accounts

- To reduce the risk of fraud by making it difficult for unauthorized transactions to be entered on the accounting system

- To reduce the risk of errors by listing transactions that are to be put on the double entry system

- To ensure that entries can be traced back to an authorized financial document

Notes

- Journal entries are prepared from authorized financial documents

- The names of the accounts to be debited and credited are listed in the details column; it is customary to show the debit transaction first

- The money amount of each debit and credit entry is stated in the appropriate column

- The reference column shows where each account is found and often includes an account number

- A journal entry always balances i.e. a debit and a credit entry are always for the same amount or total

- A narrative is usually included briefly explaining why the transaction is being carried out and making reference to the financial document

- Each journal entry is complete in itself and is ruled off to separate it from the next entry

Opening entries

Opening entries are the transactions to open the account of a new business

Payroll Transactions

Payroll transactions are the accounting entries which record wages and salaries paid t employees

Payroll transactions require journal and accounting entries for:

- Gross pay

- Net pay

- Income tax

- Employers national insurance contributions

- Employees national insurance contributions

- Employers pension contributions

- Employee's pension contributions

- Voluntary deductions from employee's pay

Payroll transactions

1) Transfer the total of payments to wages account (this is the cost to the employer) and to the wages control account

2) Make entries for the payment of wages (the net pay paid from the bank)

3) Transfer the amount due to HMRC account

4) Transfer the amount due to the pension fund

5) Transfer the amount due for voluntary deductions

The trial balance and correction of errors

A trial balance is a list of the balances from every account from the general ledger (including the cash book and petty cash book) distinguishing between those accounts which have debit balances and those which have credit balances.

Errors in the accounting system

Ways to avoid errors or ways to reveal them sooner, include:

- Division of the accounting function between a number of people, so that not one person is responsible for all aspects of a business transaction

- Regular circulation of statements of account to customers who will check the transactions of their accounts and advise of any discrepancies

- Checking the statements of accounts received from suppliers against the accounting records

- Extraction of a trial balance at regular intervals

- The checking of bank statements and preparing bank reconciliation statements

- Checking cash and petty cash balances against cash held

- The use of control accounts

- The use of a computer accounting program

Errors not disclosed by the trial balance

- **Error of omission** – both debit and credit entries have not been made

- **Error of commission** – a transaction has been entered to the wrong person's account

- **Error of principle** – a transaction has been entered in the wrong type of account

- **Error of original entry** – a transaction has been entered incorrectly in both debit and credit accounts